Priority Number One

PRIORITY
NUMBER ONE

Prioritizing The Hell ^{Ish Parts} Out Of Parenting

Crystal Zurligen

Paperback ISBN 979-8-9876788-0-0
Ebook ISBN 979-8-9876788-1-7
Audiobook ISBN 979-8-9876788-2-4

Edited by Gina DeLuca
Cover Design by Chloe Davis
Interior Design by Adam Zurligen

www.prioritynumberone.org

To my children, grand children and great grand children: I love you, look forward to meeting you, and hope that you will each experience the joy, peace and strength that comes from putting God first.

To the one (that's you): may you take responsibility for every bit of your beautiful life and learn to carry on with grace when the beauty is difficult to see.

Contents

viii   Dear Friend

x   Preface

xiv   Introduction

Chapter One

     1   No Pity

     3   Honesting Harshly

     9   Mindless Wanting

Chapter Two

     15   Wondering Why

     17   Relinquishing Control

     22   Unclear Delineation Of Limits

Chapter Three

     27   Super Human

     29   Un-Shirking Responsibilities

     33   Consistently Resorting To Immediate Self Care

Chapter Four

39   It's Okay To Be Different

41   Embodying Change

44   Forgetting That You Can Harness
Spiritual Power

Chapter Five

51   2nd Law Of Thermodynamics

53   Engineering Systems

58   Overlooking "Safety Belts"

Chapter Six

63   Don't Forget The Other Kids

65   Rotating Priorities

69   Hyper-focusing On "Fun" And "Now"

Chapter Seven

75   Grown And Gone

77   Deciphering Desires

81   Assuming They Will Catch The Drift

85   Parting Words

91   Acknowledgements

94   Works Cited

Dear Friend,

Buried within these pages you will find my naked soul. I have laid myself bare in an attempt to see clearly the tangle of yarn that is my emotions, thoughts and feelings around parenting. I have been carefully teasing apart the knots, trying to avoid making things more of a mess than they already are. I'm pretty sure that the job will never be "done," but that's okay. It's a soothing (and at times, very vexing) process nonetheless.

To be brutally honest, I am writing this book for myself. However, I wouldn't be publishing it if I weren't also writing it for you. In fact, I am going to great lengths to make this book available NOW. At this chaotic stage of my life. Why? Because of what I believe about parenting. I'll sum it up here: Parenting is possibly the most difficult endeavor we will ever face. The human trend is to avoid pain and difficulty at all costs, but, when parents are not intentional with their parenting, the whole world suffers. That effect is not immediate, but it is forthcoming.

I wrote this book because I have had a hard time being a parent. For something that is my job every minute of each and every day, I wanted to enjoy it more. Through writing, I have gained greater perspective and understanding. Through writing, I have been guided to what I needed to change about myself and my parenting in order to be a happier me. The greatest change came after I sorted out my priorities and put God at the top of my list. My pleasure from parenting has since skyrocketed, as did my confidence in it. My goal is to show you a purposeful path that you can travel to get those same results. I still have days that I would rather not repeat, and so will you, but I know that God will take your every effort and multiply it to your benefit as well as the benefit of your children.

I expect, by the end, that you will have a more clear idea of what steps you can take and changes you can make to your life in order to have a more satisfying and gratifying experience as a parent! The joy of parenting will be easier to behold after adjusting the focus of your life's lenses. Together, we can create lasting, universal change by becoming better parents.

Better Parents; Better People,
Crystal

Preface

I wake up every morning to the exciting adventure of raising small humans! Imagine narrow escapes, adrenaline hits, and things "mostly" working out in the end. Our last adventure was just a couple of days ago. I had left my wallet in Tucson, and had a limited amount of time to retrieve it before our airplane departed from Phoenix. Not a single one of us thought we were going to make it, but somehow (magically) we did. Did we run through the airport with a baby in a stroller, a three year old on Daddy's shoulders and four boys darting in and out of the crowd? Yes. Were we the last ones to board the plane before they shut the gate? Also yes. I was just excited that when we found our seats, all eight of us were present and accounted for.

The stress of everyday life as a parent of little persons is, at times, staggering. Often, I find myself grasping for something, anything, that will help me not feel so vulnerable.

I saw a video of a father taking time to be with his two-year-old daughter. She was in the middle of an epic tantrum. There was kicking, screaming, and crying while dad sat supporting her through the experience. While it was definitely inspiring, I also felt discouraged. I have six children. SIX hooligans under the age of twelve. There are so many things that I have to get done in a day and so many people's needs to be aware of; it doesn't seem likely that I would ever be able to offer that kind of support to a single child.

I have been listening to parenting podcasts, reading parenting books and taking parenting courses. Every time I come away with new things to try, but there are always parts that I don't agree with or pieces that don't really fit my family. Usually I give up after something doesn't work, compare myself to all the other parents out there, and then I fall. Overwhelm is the pit I usually land in, which, on occasion, has led to deeper, darker emotions. I decided that I needed a book that would strengthen my core, and that I should write it myself.

When I was a teenager I started writing letters. I wrote them to my future husband, my future kids[1] and my future self. The earliest ones are irritatingly adolescent, but I see that they were a way for me to keep my hopes and dreams close when they seemed so far away. Even now, when I am frustrated and overwhelmed I pull out a pen and some paper and start

---

[1] I know that a kid is technically a baby goat. While baby goats *are* super cute, I will be using the term "kid" to refer to human children.

to write. Addressing my fears, concerns and emotions in this way has been an invaluable exercise for this stage of my parenting, so I decided to include several letters.

You will also encounter seven prioritization steps. These steps are designed to progressively bring mindfulness to your current lifestyle. This will help you understand what things make parenting so difficult, and give you ideas on what you can do about it.

I also knew that I needed to confront several of the parenting hazards that I have noticed and make my own plans to avoid them. These are potential problems that we need to be conscious of because many good parents fall into these traps and stay there. Each chapter will contain a letter written to myself, a prioritization step for you to take as well as a parent trap to be aware of and avoid.

I hope that reading this book will inspire you to take a look at the life you have created and choose to improve upon it. You have the power to significantly decrease the frequency of hellish experiences that you go through as a parent. You will be more satisfied, more comfortable and more joyful as you create positive change within yourself through the process of prioritization. The world will be a better place and your children will be better too. They need to watch you try. They need to see you exhibit what it is to fail but not lose. And, yeah, you are going to fail (probably often), but that's okay! You are the best *you* when failure no longer keeps you from continuing to strive.

Introduction:
Parenting is Hard

Don't get me wrong, I'm totally with you, and so are the 73% of Americans who say that parenting is their *biggest* challenge[2]. I also recognize that hard is GOOD. Hard helps people progress. Hard makes people work, it brings out the best in us and it *can* be awesome. Except when it's not, and believe me, I've been there.

I've had times of simply surviving my parenting journey (let alone enjoying it), I've dealt with chronic overwhelm and frustration, and I've had months of being physically present but not emotionally there. I've felt the heavy burden of raising good kids, and I've seen how in so many cases I haven't used the "hard" to inspire progress.

Maybe you have no idea what I'm talking about since your kids are squishy cherubs, but I'm guessing

---

[2] "Tuning in: National Parent Survey Report" Zero To Three, Accessed Jan 28, 2023, https://www.zerotothree.org/wp-content/uploads/2022/10/National-Parent-Survey-Report.pdf

that most people who have taken on the child rearing challenge have had some of these same experiences.

Where do you currently fall on the emotional spectrum of parents?

1. Parenting is the worst and I may or may not hate my offspring.
2. I'm losing it. Patience, hair, mojo... you name it.
3. "One of those days" happened six times this week.
4. Why can't I catch a break?
5. Meh.
6. Got quite a few kinks to work out.
7. Things are looking up.
8. Loving this gig even though it's tough.
9. Nailing it 90% of the time.
10. Could not be better!

Hard isn't positive or negative. What we do with the hard, though, can have a compelling effect in either direction. Acknowledging where you currently stand is the first step of turning difficulty into a positive force for your life.

This book is designed to help you with the steps that come after that. Every prioritization step and parent trap will have a "Take Action" section at the end with questions to ask yourself or activities to complete. You can do these exercises mentally, of course, but your improvement will be easier to see over time if you write your answers out in a journal or notebook. Personally, I suggest snatching the nearest empty spiral notebook you can find and dedicating it to your parenting journey. Having a set aside space for this process will also help you take yourself seriously, so go on, grab a notebook and let's get started!

Chapter 1

Dear Crystal,

In case you hadn't noticed…You don't get paid for being a mom. Earlier today when you finished cleaning the kitchen, you texted a group of your neighborhood mom-friends knowing that their responses might be the only recognition you would get. The slow-clap gif was all it took to make you feel like you'd done good, so all is right in the world, yeah?

News Flash: Adam[3] doesn't get paid to be a dad either. In today's societal climate where, "money won't buy you happiness, but it will buy you a boat,"[4] we have difficulty focusing our time and energy on things that don't further us along that particular "happiness" track. We don't get paid to raise kids (unless you count the child-tax-credit…which I don't). We don't even get a bonus if they turn out nice. What the heck?!

---

[3] Adam is my favorite (and only) husband.

[4] Janson, Chris. "Buy Me A Boat." Track 1 on *Buy Me A Boat*. Warner Records, 2015, CD.

Chapter 1

Well, I'm writing you a book so you'll remember. Remember to take this work seriously no matter how forlorn the path may seem. No amount of money would be enough to compensate you for all that you do, and interestingly, the rewards that you do get aren't anything that money could buy. It's time to prioritize. It's also time to get over it. If you expect credit, compensation, recognition or rewards for doing what you do…you, my friend, are in for a life of disappointment.

The time is now. Be amazing because that's what you want to be! Be on top of your life because you feel so much better when you are. Figure it out because you'll be happier with yourself when you do. Remember that success, like beauty, is in the eye of the beholder. If you want to feel accomplished as a parent, beholding your purpose from a grander perspective and moving toward that design will help you to get there.

Love,
Me

Prioritization Step: Honesting Harshly

It's time for us to be more honest. I'm thinking of one person in particular that you should be brutally truthful with. No, it's not your mother (she probably wouldn't like that anyway). This person is the one who wields the tools that make your days what they are. This person is responsible for the things that happen *in* you. This is the person who decides what you think, what you wear and how you act (or react). Let me introduce you: _____ meet _____.
<small>(insert your name)</small>   <small>(insert your name again)</small>

Yep, *you* are the one that you need to be honest with.

Honesting harshly (being harshly honest with yourself) is the key that unlocks the door of progress. You still have work to do after this door is unlocked… but it's a huge step.

Often, we beat ourselves up about not doing all the things we had planned for the day. We feel discouraged because we took our kids places that they needed to go, made them a good meal, folded two loads of laundry and even practiced the piano, but we didn't get to mowing the lawn or reorganizing the front closet. Other times we "scroll" the day away, not doing any of the things that we had intended to accomplish, then baby ourselves into believing that we just needed the day off. We need to stop building ourselves up illegitimately and beating ourselves down unnecessarily. We need to take ourselves as we are in truth.

Here's where I'm at today: I haven't done two loads of laundry, I've washed and dried three. None of them are put away yet, but I did clear some of the piles left over from last time. I have not really connected with my children in meaningful ways or done activities with them. We've talked in passing and I've consoled them when necessary, but, for the most part, they've been on their own. I've been focused on laundry (still not done, but I've got time left today, it's only 5:30 p.m.). I made it on time to work for both shifts (I'm a crossing guard), but I'm really feeling rather blah.

Honesting harshly can be a bit uncomfortable, and it takes mental work, but I know that in the end, it helps the "blah" transform into the results that I want. If I'm being honest, I remind myself that I'm not proud of all the Easter candy that I've eaten today. If I'm being honest, I remind myself that the day is not over and that I still have time to intentionally connect. If I'm being honest, I let myself remember that I have to choose one or two or maybe three priorities (of many) to focus on today, and the others I will pick up tomorrow. If I'm being honest, I will use this moment to gather myself together and decide what change(s) to make.

Change doesn't always have to be big and scary. Right now, I think I will change just one thing. I'm going to leave this room with a little spring in my step and I'm going to focus on the things that I had set out to do today. Laundry and connect.

Let's just say that by the end of today even though I did make that change, I did not finish the laundry. I might be tempted to fall into bed and cry because I didn't finish one of just two things that I really wanted to do. I might also be tempted to leave the clean clothes there for a few more days until the next time that laundry needs doing and just deal with the ramifications (more work for me). It's ok to say, "Self, we could have done better—let's try harder tomorrow." But it's also ok to say, "You know, I didn't finish folding, but I did connect with each kid. I'll make sure to put the clothes away before they wake up in the morning." I think in this case I'll say them both.

When I look at the world I am living in through the lens of "honesting harshly," I see that many parents have let go of their responsibility to teach. During the 2021/2022 school year, the majority of American school-aged children (around 95%)[5] were in public, private or charter schools. While I do consider educational institutions to be a blessing (my kids attend public school), I see how sending our children away to receive their formal education has blurred the lines between who should be teaching what.

If I am harshly honest I see that currently, we, as a society, might be *avoiding* teaching and parenting our children. We often default to putting them in front of the TV or handing them an iPad because that's easier than interacting on a personal level and enforcing boundaries and rules. We are using all sorts of excuses to escape our responsibilities and duties because, surprise, surprise—It's hard. This is the current that will take us down-stream to a Niagara-like waterfall. I'm pretty sure I can count on one hand the people who have taken that trip and survived[6]; It's time for us to climb out of the river and face the parenting mountain.

---

[5] Brian D Ray. "How Many Homeschool Students Are There In The United States During the 2021-2022 School Year?" National Home Education Research Institute. September 15, 2022, https://www.nheri.org/how-many-homeschool-students-are-there-in-the-united-states-during-the-2021-2022-school-year/).

[6] "List of people who have gone over Niagra Falls" Wikipedia, Accessed Jan 28, 2023, https://en.wikipedia.org/wiki/List_of_people_who_have_gone_over_Niagara_Falls
(Apparently fifteen people are recorded to have been over the falls and survived. I stand corrected.)

Funny story… As I'm typing this, I realize that I escaped to my office to write *because* I was feeling frustrated by my children and wanted to get away. Guess what? I for sure feel better right now! Of course I do. I am no longer part of the dinner time chaos of our family of eight. If I can write long enough, I might even sneak my way out of bed time!

All jokes aside, all I really did was put up an umbrella to shield me from the downpour instead of fixing the leak in the ceiling. When we eat breakfast tomorrow, my children will likely display the same attitudes and mannerisms that they did tonight because I made absolutely no effort to correct behaviors or exemplify good ones. I disappeared with an exasperated huff. It's time for me to get out of the river–I'll just be helping Adam get the kids to bed—give me a sec.

Take Action

Here are two Honesting Harshly help questions. **Write the answers to these questions at the end of each day to get a more realistic view of the good that you are doing as well as the improvements that you need to make.**

What did you do today that made you feel accomplished?

What did you do (or not do) today that you would have preferred to have done differently?

Parent Trap: Mindless Wanting

Everyone has experienced mindless wanting. Remember the time when your mom handed you a toy catalog and asked you to circle what you wanted for Christmas? Remember how you handed it back to her and there were at least fifty things that you *really* wanted? Remember how she never went that route again? Our world is designed to make us want stuff. My friend from Germany remarked on her recent visit: "Man! Americans are good at marketing!"

I've never lived outside of the United States of America but the commercial nature of our society isn't hard to miss. I've seen and experienced how a certain color can remind me of my favorite restaurant, and how my kids constantly want whatever they see. There's nothing wrong with wanting things, but when we aren't aware of it, mindless wanting will lead to discontent.

Just two days ago I fell prey to this trap. I took my oldest son to meet up with my brother and sister-in-law for lunch. I was hungry and ordered what I wanted: a chicken sandwich. My son got a footlong hot dog, ice cream and fries. When the cashier asked if we wanted anything else, my eye flew back to the menu and immediately landed on...sweet potato fries. Without even blinking, I said, "Oh yes, we'll take some sweet potato fries."

Hey, if I was craving it, then I must have needed some of the nutrients from the sweet potatoes, right? Well, this was the outcome. I overate. I ate those sweet potato fries even though they weren't as yummy as I wanted them to be. I ate my whole chicken sandwich, which was delicious, and then I helped my son with his ice cream and fries. We took the leftovers home and ended up throwing them away. None of this is a terrible problem, it's just that I made a mindless choice that wasn't in alignment with my overall lifestyle goals. The few extra dollars, the few extra calories, and writing my mindlessness off as a phenomenon of pregnancy are all seemingly inconsequential expenses to pay. But what would my life become if I were to live this way day after day?

That cashier and every other cashier out there has been trained to ask that very question at the end of every order in order to exploit our mindless wanting. This can be problematic because mindless wanting can lead to a life of meaningless frivolity. When we live our lives according to the ever changing direction of the breeze, we find that we travel aimlessly and without purpose. It is time to get real with ourselves and our children about the world that we live in; a world where you can potentially have whatever you want whenever you want it with the swipe of a card or the touch of a button. We ought to be preparing them for what they are really up against.

Marketing has infiltrated every area of our lives, so there are many opportunities for us to overcome mindless wanting. For example, we all have to take time to go to the grocery store, and don't always get to do it child-free. We have also all experienced the "pester power" that a diligent child wields, and understand how exhausting that power can be! Next time you go out for groceries with a child, make sure they know before you enter the store if they will get a treat or not–and then stick with it (even if the doughnuts are on sale). You might even want to consider taking them to an actual grocery store rather than an everything store so that there aren't as many potential items for them to salivate over. Go in with an actual list of things that you have previously decided to purchase; if it's not on the list, then don't buy it.

What does giving in to our mindless wanting teach our children? What are the core beliefs that they are developing because of it? Do they think that they should have whatever they want? Is that attitude any fun for you when you inevitably have to take them to the grocery store? How can we help them become aware of their own mindless wanting?

Take Action

Next time you want something, take a moment to ask yourself these questions:

Is this something that I (as in my conscious thinking self) actually want, or just something someone else wants me to want? Does this choice support my long term goals and desires?

Take every chance you can get to prepare your children for a lifetime of making intentional choices:

If a kid needs to go buy a toy for a sibling or friend, help them decide beforehand what their budget is and what kind of item they are looking for.

Don't fail to remind them of the things you previously decided when they inevitably get distracted.

Talk about marketing and help your kids recognize it.

Avoid video and internet content that has advertising directed toward children.

Help them recognize when they have given into their wants without thinking, and encourage them to be more intentional next time!

Chapter 2

Dear Crystal,

Remember the day you were supposed to fly to California for a siblings and spouses only trip? The plan was to enjoy two days child-free at the happiest place on earth, but the results of your covid test that morning positively messed with your schedule. I imagine you haven't forgotten it, I remember as if it were yesterday. Wait. What time is it? 12:03 a.m. Okay, yeah. That was yesterday.

I'm writing this letter to remind you (and me) that it's going to be all right in the end. The reasons why things happen the way they do don't really matter. If it already happened—it happened already! Nothing you say, do, or think will change what or how things went down. You have learned that your mind is much less conflicted when you choose to face the future instead of hide from it behind wishes about the past.

At this moment I believe that not going on the trip was best but I don't feel like I have to be happy about it. I'm mourning the loss of time spent with loved ones. I'm grieving over the death of my excitement and anticipation. The overwhelming emotion of the day has been "sad." The awesome thing though, is that I'm not wondering why.

"Why?", right now, would be a waste of energy. "What if I had or hadn't?" would get my mind going, but to where? Those thoughts would be speculation and they wouldn't change a thing. Sure, additional understanding would be nice…but not actually necessary. The important thing to ask yourself is, "what am I going to do about it now?" If there's nothing to be done then try, "what can I learn from this experience to improve outcomes the next time things don't go as planned?"

I'm hoping that you'll remember this for struggles small and big. Remember, it's okay to choose sad, and there's no shame in grief. When things don't work out, let yourself feel and when you're all feel'd out—move on.

For the day when things just aren't going your way, direct your mind to your blessings. Trust that there are many reasons why (most of which are probably to your benefit) and that you might never know what those reasons are. Not a problem. Also, remember that anger curses no one but you. It will all be right in the end, you'll see.

Love,
Me

Prioritization Step: Relinquishing Control

Let's get real here: There will *always* be things that are arduous about trying to influence the people that we have charge over. Why is it hard? Because we don't have any *actual* control over them. Charge over—Yes. Control over—No. It feels like we do, or at least like we *should* have a little control over our children but it's just not true. Children have to make their own choices and have their own experiences in order to learn and grow. Their behaviors and choices are exasperating when we allow ourselves to think (or even wish) that we are in control.

So if we don't have control over our children, then what are we striving for? Do we actually want them to be perfect? Do we want them to get their homework finished at any cost? Or, are we willing to allow them to forget and experience the natural consequences of their actions? If we can't control their every move, then why do we often allow their choices to determine our own attitudes and experiences as parents?

Chapter 2

One night, in my college days, I went to a church singles event. One of my peers asked this question: "Why do we experience adversity in life?"

Well, no one offered a response, and things were starting to feel awkward, so I said, "We have to know what it is to be miserable in order to know what it is to be happy." I thought it was a sound answer and was therefore surprised when he responded, "No. That's wrong."

I felt immediately indignant, which made his follow-up statement all the more poignant:

"Adversity is mandatory. Misery is not."

In that moment I realized that I had been allowing myself to dwell in all sorts of unpleasant emotions. More importantly, I understood that much of what I was going through at the time was not a "requirement" of my life in that season. I had been telling myself to be patient, and that everything would improve, but I wasn't doing much to drag myself out of the wallowing. I was allowing my circumstances (mostly things that were out of my control) to determine my attitude toward life, and it wasn't to my advantage. I understand that we will all experience misery (and that it does, in fact, help us recognize joy), but we don't have to stay in misery—that part is a choice.

Reflecting on this moment has helped me to understand one of the reasons why I have, at times, been unhappy with parenthood: I am miserable when I am trying to control what I can't. Letting go of the assumption that we should have more control over our surroundings will drastically reduce our levels of stress. Are we going to be frustrated? Yeah. Have times where we feel annoyed or even angry? Yep. But, relinquishing control of the things that you don't have power over will make room for taking charge of the one person that you *can* control: yourself.

You Can't Control	You Can Control
Inconsiderate drivers	Your reaction to them
Change	How you adapt to it
The attitude of your kid	Your attitude about your kid
Other people's opinions	Your own opinions
The weather	How prepared you are for it
Other people's tantrums	Your response to them
The food your children eat	What you put on their plates

Aside from putting more stress on ourselves by trying to control things that we can't, when it comes to our children, we are actually doing them a disservice when we carry their responsibilities for them. Kids need every opportunity to practice being independent. In other words, they should have as much control over their own lives as they are capable of handling. However, catering to their every whim does not equal giving them control. What I'm suggesting is that we create ways to allow them to exercise their own power. At the very least, we should not interfere with the consequences that are tied to their actions and *support* them when they falter or fail.

Take Action

Make a list of things that you can't control but have been trying to.

Come up with a plan for reminding yourself to relinquish things that are not in your control.

Write out the answers to these questions:

What things can you do to create opportunities for your children to be more independent?

What areas of your own life would you like to be more intentional about?

Parent Trap:
Unclear Delineation of Limits

My grandpa says that kids these days are confused because their limits are not clearly delineated (he's a psychologist). When I say that you need to let your kid have his own power, I am *not* saying that you need to let him do whatever he wants. I am definitely not saying that you should let him walk all over you. The best way to responsibly allow your children to have their own power is to give them clear parameters within which to operate.

If you've ever been to a zoo, you know that the fences, barriers, protocols and procedures all serve an important purpose: to keep everyone safe (aka alive). The bars at the zoo may seem akin to a prison, but without them, the zoo would be quite unsafe.

When we fail to clearly outline boundaries, limits, expectations and rules with our children, they are in danger of more than just being eaten.

One family standard that we stick to is that no one under the age of eight is allowed to wield a pocket knife. Toddlers and very young children do not have the dexterity required to safely use very sharp objects.

Their brains are not developed enough to understand the serious consequences that can result from misusing a knife. Around age seven, we begin training with a knife and at age eight, if our child has demonstrated a proper amount of respect for the tool, we allow them to have their first pocket knife. If I were to authorize my three-year-old to have his own sharp knife, the exact consequences would be difficult to foresee. I'd probably have a holier couch, but the effects could be much more grievous.

A pocket knife is a physical tool and therefore needs physical boundaries. Staying out of the operator's "blood circle" (the arm's length area around a person holding a knife), transferring the tool to another person handle first and never cutting towards yourself are all examples of boundaries that should be set for this particular tool.

Boundaries like these are needed in all areas of our children's lives. Being capable of exercising control within limits is a valuable skill that will serve your child the rest of his or her life. Think of someone who has been taught to operate within the limit of being kind. Being capable of telling the truth while still being considerate of others won't only help your child succeed, it will also make the world a better place.

Kids don't just need you to set limits, they need your consistency in upholding them. My friend Cheryl shared this story with me:

"We had an Ayrshire milk cow. Everyday, we'd let her out of the barn after milking her and she would walk the entire edge of the fence to see if by chance there was a way she could get out. Over time, she developed this habit, just checking the fences. If there was one wire down, she would get out. And if there's one wire down, those kids will take it. They're checking the fence to see if it's still up. Is the rule still the same today as it was yesterday?"

I'll admit, it's exhausting to eat dinner as a family when you are trying to set limits and be consistent! "No burping at the table!" "Don't chew with your mouth open!" "Please! Say please!" The time for delineation was actually before the table was set. If the expectation to have good manners has previously been established, acknowledging a belch at the table with eye contact and a raised eyebrow may be enough of a reminder that the fence is still up.

Take Action

Identify a specific boundary that you have already established in your home.

Is this boundary difficult to enforce? When did you set up this boundary? Does this fence need to be put back in place or do any clarifications need to be made? Are your expectations for this boundary realistic? Are the consequences reasonable?

Think of an area of life that would be benefited by having more clearly outlined limits, and then take the time to set up the boundaries.

Chapter 3

Dear Crystal,

I know you feel like you need to be "supermom" for all the people who depend on you. Children don't understand the effort that goes into putting food on their plates, keeping their clothes clean, and maintaining a general semblance of order in the home. Those things alone are a lot to keep track of, and they aren't even your only responsibilities.

Many days you find that you have fallen short. By a long shot.

It's okay. Think of yourself as Mrs. Incredible! In today's case: Mrs. Incredibly Impatient. On other days, Mrs. Incredibly Slothish or Petty. Do you feel unequal to the tasks before you? Whichever prevailing emotion you feel today: Just Keep Going. What good does it do to worry? You are a human. So human you might even call yourself super human. And that's not a bad thing! When you have an extra human day, just know that it's part of who you are right now! Guess what? Every single person that you have ever met or even glanced at is in that very same boat. We are all subject to the ebbs and flows, the ups and downs, the highs and lows! You being in the trough all of a sudden when you're pretty sure you were cresting just moments earlier doesn't make you a hypocrite, just human.

When you recognize that you have fallen, pick yourself up! Start moving, if you feel that you just can't...Help will always be given to those who ask.

Being human isn't all bad,
Crystal

Prioritization Step: Un-shirking Responsibilities

Lately I've been thinking about the police department. I'm a crossing guard and have noticed the many flashing blue and red lights as people continue to speed through the school zone while I'm on the job. I've been feeling grateful that we are all working together to create a safe space for kids to walk to and away from school. I was hired by my city police department to help protect people (no matter how small) and maintain order. When I took the job, I was given all the tools that I would need in order to be a decent guard. This included a handheld stop sign, traffic cones, and a neon green reflective vest. I also received a clearly outlined job description to refer to, and phone numbers to call should I run into any difficulties.

I realized that though parenting is my most significant job, I've only been given a few physical tools and I don't have an official description of what it is exactly that I'm supposed to be doing! I understand why there's not a super specific manual available or a one-size-fits-all ideal to strive for, but I believe that we will be more confident and capable parents if we are willing to un-shirk our responsibilities.

First, we need to know what our responsibilities are. Second, we need to gather the tools that we will need in order to do a decent job. Third, we need to accept that no one can do the first and second steps for us. Those are things we have to figure out for ourselves.

When I think of all the things I'm responsible for, I want to hide in my closet and cry. The other day, while trying to sort all this parenting business out, I grabbed a sheet of paper and began writing down all the things that I consider to be my parenting responsibilities.

Some of the things on my list had to do with responsibilities outside my home, like my crossing guard duties and church assignments. Some were not actually my responsibilities at all, like making sure that school backpacks are hung on their respective hooks. When I removed these things and others like them, I had a pretty good list of my parenting duties.

I realized that I could simplify my long list into three different categories:

Teach
Correct
Demonstrate

First, my job is to teach my children. I teach them to walk, talk, eat, play, clean the toilets, be responsible, recognize the signs of depression, and more. If I don't teach them, then their dad will, and I'm not sure he knows the right way to clean a toilet! (Just kidding, Adam is a really great house cleaner) The point is, that the responsibility of educating my children is mine. Assuming or hoping that someone else will teach them for me is shirking my responsibilities.

Second, it is my duty to correct or *teach them over and over again*. Take my four year old as an example. I taught him how to wipe his bottom (you guys can handle this example, right?), but I can't rely on a one time five minute lesson to do the trick. He's going to need some correction in order to make sure that his little buns are clean. I've had to teach it, let him practice it, and teach it again/correct. Sometimes I forget that people (big and small) learn things at different speeds. I need to just relax a little and teach again, rather than stress over the fact that "I taught this lesson already!" and "Why didn't he remember?"

Third, I have to demonstrate. This means consistently attempting to live my life in accordance with the principles that my husband and I want our children to learn. If we are doing our best to teach compassion and respect, practicing what we preach gives us credibility. Neither of us is perfect, so when we fail we teach them through demonstration what to do when they fail. Acknowledging that what we did was not in harmony with what we want and then doing better the next time will help them just as much (if not more) than never speaking a disrespectful word.

Teaching, correcting and demonstrating are all essential parts of our parenting responsibilities. However, even diligence in each category does not guarantee satisfactory results in our children. Those results are not ours to control. The awesome thing about un-shirking our responsibilities is that we get the satisfaction that comes from a job well done.

Take Action

Write down the things you are responsible for as a parent.

Are there any things on the list that you should relinquish? How can you simplify this list to make it more manageable?

Write your own parenting job description.

Parent Trap:
Resorting to Immediate Self Care

I often have days where things don't go quite according to plan (it doesn't take six kids to make this a reality). The baby has a blowout when we are already running late. A kid traces his hand on the wall with magenta crayon—twice. The laundry piles up and no one has clean underwear, or my messy home is too overwhelming to even think about. When I am having a hard day and tell a friend about it, a common response is "Wow. You need to take a break! You should have Adam watch the kids for a long time so that you can go do whatever you want. Get out of the house, get a massage, be away from your children and just reset."

To be clear, there's nothing wrong with any of those options. Maybe a resort is exactly what I need! We have to take care of ourselves in order to perform at the highest level we are capable of. Just as we have different parts of ourselves that need caring for, there are different types of self care. A simple online search will tell you that people have many different ideas about self care. You can do your own research there if you'd like. I'm going to go simple and say that there are two types of self to care for:

Your *immediate* self and your *future* self.

Your immediate self is the part of you that deals with right now. It's the short term you that wants relief and gratification. Immediate self care is not a crime. It can be fun, and it can give you just the boost you need in order to carry on. Immediate self care addresses personal needs that are right in front of you.

"Future you" self care is different. It's often forgotten because it's not as shiny and enticing. Future self care is more concerned with ensuring the happiness and sanity of future you, and it almost always requires effort. Anything that can be done now that will make later you have an easier go of it would be considered future self care.

I have a friend who is very serious about her dinner prep each day. She knows that her 5 p.m. self is going to be exhausted—such is life with her particular chronic illness. She knows that the last thing in the world her 5:00 self will want to think about is what to make for dinner. Every morning after dropping her children off for school, she comes home and gets things ready for dinner while she still has the energy to do so. This is one example of future self care.

Here are some examples of things you can do to care for your immediate self and future self:

Immediate self care:
Taking a bubble bath
Taking a break from the children
Journaling or thought work
Watching television or movies
Exercise
Getting a massage
Eating ice cream after a hard day
Anything that gives short-term relief from your cares

Future self care:
Meal prepping
Setting goals and making plans
Budgeting
Planning your day the night before
Setting out your next day's clothes
Exercise
Journaling or thought-work
Making sure kitchen table is cleaned before bed

Some self care practices can fall under both categories, and some self care practices may switch categories depending on what your goals and dreams are. Future self care items don't have to feel like chores.

When you know where you are going and why, looking into the future feels like less of a drag. When you get good at it, you'll find that you enjoy it just as much as immediate self care because you are making things so much easier for future you.

Consistently resorting to immediate self care can actually damage our attitudes toward parenting and children. For example: I love reading. It's a wonderful hobby that enriches my life. A few years ago I realized that I was *completely* ignoring my children and husband so that I could use every available moment to participate in this particular form of "self care". Adam would come home from school to find that I had been reading on the couch all day. Dishes—dirty. Laundry—in piles around the house. Children—starved for attention. I was taking something that filled my bucket and consistently using it to avoid and distract me from my greatest responsibilities. When the kids would come asking me to read to them or play I would be annoyed and brush them off. When I finished reading a great book…all I wanted was my next quick fix.

I was reading in the name of "self care" but it was all in vain. Abusing self care in this manner turned something good and beautiful essentially into a drug. I had become addicted to the feel goods that came from escaping my responsibilities and filling my wants. The trouble was that while I did enjoy temporary relief from my cares, I wasn't addressing the problems that were causing me to need relief in the first place.

Using self care selfishly can have devastating effects. True self care encompasses our responsibilities, because they are part of us. There's nothing wrong with taking care of our immediate needs. But when immediate self care is the only type that we participate in, our long term needs will be the same tomorrow and the next day and the day after that. In order to stop the cycle of overwhelm, future self care is imperative.

Take Action

Make a list of your favorite immediate self care practices:

Evaluate this list. Why do you participate in them? What do they accomplish for you? How often do you do them?

Now identify some new self care items that you know your future self will appreciate.

Schedule this future self care. If you don't feel like you have time, try combining one of your immediate self care go-to's with a future self care practice.

Chapter 4

Dear Crystal,

Sometimes it is stressful to go against the grain…you worry about what people think and you feel like whatever you are doing is uncharted territory. Moving forward seems uncertain, and many times it is tempting to stay as you are, where you are, doing what you do.

Remember the last couple years of Adam's undergrad? That apartment was TINY. There were two bedrooms…but it was a tight squeeze for the two of you and three little boys. Every time one of the children took a nap, the other two would have to bring any books and toys that they wanted to read or play with into the small living room. Of course, that meant that all 900 of our square feet were overcome with the shenanigans of the young and the restless.

Finally, you couldn't take it anymore and knew that something would have to be done differently in order for your sanity to come out of hiding.

That's when you created "the sleeping room." You tucked the queen bed into the closet, put the crib in one corner and a bunk bed in the other. The clothes, toys and books all went in the second bedroom with a play area on the other side of the credenza. It worked marvelously! Nap time no longer meant that the rest of our space would be overwhelmed. The kids just played in the "everything else" room while the baby slept.

It was definitely unusual, but a raised eyebrow eventually stopped giving you anxiety. You saw the benefit of doing what you could with the resources that you had regardless of what you thought others might think of the situation.

Please remember. There's no need to do things the way other people do them. Awesome people are awesome because they are doing things the way that **they** would do them. They are successful because they aren't afraid to be themselves.

You are the only person like you out there, so yeah! You're going to be unique, which is amazing! Please, don't think about what you think other people will think. It's exhausting and likely not true anyway. Just do the best you can with what you've got and things will work out fine.

Love,
Me

Prioritization Step: Embodying Change

One of my favorite things in the world is water. I love watching water crash against a shore and love admiring its accumulations in the sky. I love to dance in a downpour or jump into the lake head first. I love how the gentle flow of a stream smooths away the jagged edges of stone, and I love the fact that everything depends upon it.

Water is constantly changing forms, and change is wrought upon everything that feels its touch. If I could give change a physical form, it would be water.

Change is the only thing that won't go away—ever, why do we resist it so?

The other night, while singing my kids to sleep, one of my children was trying to stifle his sobs. I wasn't aware of any incident, so I climbed into bed with him and asked what was going on. He said he was feeling sad because he was missing his home. We moved a few months ago, so it's natural for him to be missing his friends, family and previous school. The painful feelings he was experiencing were related to his thought response to the change. "If Covid hadn't happened then we would still be in Moses Lake." "I wish I could go back and live there again." "I don't have as many friends here as I did there." "I knew my old school better and never got lost."

I'm using him as an example because we can all relate. We know what it is to pine after something that no longer exists, and we have all experienced the heartache that so often comes with change. My son was spinning out in his thoughts which made it difficult for him to accept his new home.

Do we have times in our parenting when we spin out in the same relentless types of thoughts? What about, "My kid used to be so compassionate, and now she's just terrible!" Or, "Life was so much easier when they were little." Or, "I wish that I hadn't been so unkind this morning." All of a sudden, we are living in the past, with no forward motion. Imagine what we could accomplish if we tweaked those thoughts so that we no longer felt resentment and shame. Try approaching these changes with curiosity instead: "My kid is having a hard time, I wonder what I can do to support her better?" Or, "These new challenges are interesting, how can I stay ahead of the game?" Or, "I was a little short with the kids this morning, is there something in particular stressing me out? What can I do about it?"

The desired outcome of change is growth and progress, but it only comes if we can be fluid like water.

When we resist change, or are rigid around it, then we are the ones who end up broken. Rather than just embracing it, what if we were to embody it? What if we sought out new ways to progress and flow thereby creating the change necessary to surge us forward? We can be fluid by improving ourselves rather than waiting with dread for change to crash down on us.

Take Action

Write out several of the things that you do as a parent that you wish you wouldn't.

Why would you like these things to be handled differently?

What can you do instead?

Parent Trap:
Forgetting That You Can Harness Spiritual Power

There is spiritual power available to us all. Perhaps you have felt it before. Maybe you have no idea what got you through that troublesome time, or were strong when you didn't think it possible. Those may have been times when the strength you had was not entirely your own.

You can harness spiritual power to win the war against the dishes, or keep your temper in check while engaging with a stubborn toddler. You can harness this power to strengthen you when the unimaginable occurs, or when you are just having a hard time. Essentially, you can harness this power to have strength through change. But how, you ask?

Well, that's a great question.

One of my favorite scriptures of all time is Proverbs 3:5-6. I love it because when I dissect it, I see a recipe for harnessing spiritual power.

"Trust in the Lord with all thine heart and lean not unto thine own understanding.
In all thy ways acknowledge him, and He shall direct thy paths."

Trust Him with all your heart:

There are many things that people believe about God, but for the purposes of trusting Him, I choose to believe that He is good. I choose to believe that He loves me unconditionally and wants me to be happy. I choose to believe that He tells the truth and will keep His promises. In fact, I expect Him to. Banking on His promises is the foundation of my faith and hope.

Rely on God's understanding:

Another thing I choose to believe about God is that He actually is omniscient. When I believe this, in conjunction with all the things that help me trust Him, knowing that His ways are higher than mine[7] is no longer a struggle. My knowledge is limited by mortality–I don't see the end from the beginning like He does–so I choose to believe that He's got the master plan and it's all under control.

---

[7] Isaiah 55:9

Acknowledge Him in all your ways:

Saying formal prayers is one way that I acknowledge Him, but when I am out and about or in the middle of something I don't always have the luxury of being able to drop to my knees and pray.

If my best friend were to walk in and I didn't have time to chat, I'd acknowledge her, right? I'd give a smile and wave, or a nod and a wink-kissy face. Something to let her know that I saw her, that I care for and appreciate her, and that I haven't forgotten her. I might even just invite her to whatever activity I was rushing off to so that we can have more time together.

I like to think about God in the same way. When I don't have time for a prayer, but want to acknowledge Him in all my ways, there are some things that I do to metaphorically "give a nod to God." These things don't take a whole lot of time or effort, but they let Him know that I remember Him, that I appreciate what he has done for me, and that I am looking for His support and strength.

When I move on to a new activity, I put God on top of whatever the venture is. For example, when I do household chores, I like to listen to an audio-book or podcast to help pass the time. In an effort to acknowledge God in that task, I will often listen to a chapter of scripture or some other spiritually uplifting audio content before turning on my exciting murder mystery. If I am headed out to go for a run or play a few games of pickleball I might just lift my eyes as I walk out and invite Him to come along with a quick "Come with me?"

Acknowledging Him doesn't have to be formal, but it should be intentional. Something (anything) that will let God know (and help you remember) what place He holds in your heart.

Be directed by God:

Thing is, when you are doing the first parts of the recipe, you know that He is directing your path!

A few years back, I was driving alone and feeling frustrated. I was vehemently explaining to God why I was unhappy about a meeting that I had just attended. It had felt pointless for me to be there, I wanted to make sure that God knew how I felt, so I told Him. After I was done venting I turned on the car radio. I hit search and just waited as it rolled through the stations—twice. When it finally landed on a channel, I heard the voice of an evangelical preacher. He said in his very southern accent,

"If you think you can ask God to sit next to you and help you through whatever it is that you're experiencing—if you think He's gonna copilot you through this life…Then you've got it all wrong! If God's on your plane, He is the *pilot*."

I turned the radio off and thanked heaven for that southern minister and the clear and direct message. I like to think that I live my life in a way that God can speak to me and I'll listen. But sometimes He has to be a little more obvious. The message that he sent me that day was that I could trust the pilot of my life. He reminded me that in that moment I was leaning on my own understanding instead of His.

When we trust Him with all our hearts, rely on His understanding and acknowledge Him in all that we do, we don't have to wonder if He is walking with us. We don't need to analyze the daily ups and downs to determine whether or not the hand of God can be found. If we have a good thought, we act on it, trusting that everything good comes from God and that the Pilot knows which direction is best. When things don't work out the way we think they should, we remind ourselves that not every minute of every day is meant to be sunshine and lollipops. The downs are just as important as the ups, and we know where to go to harness the power that will help carry us through.

Take Action

Write down your answers to these questions:

Are there any areas of your life that you feel you could be trusting God more on?

What are some ways that you can acknowledge God in your daily doings?

Make a list of changes are you trying to make that you could use additional strength for.

Determine how you will harness available spiritual power to make it happen.

Chapter 5

Dear Crystal,

You are the lucky duck who got married to an engineer who studied physics. This means you know a little bit more than you would like to know about thermodynamics.

Let's talk about the second law of thermo. Remember what happens when you leave a system alone for a while? Think of the house: when you are not there to prevent certain young people from running amok, it doesn't take long before things are in a state of disarray. Clothing and toys will be strewn about, food will be in miscellaneous corners, and as you walk through wondering what happened, probably you'll step in something wet.

This deterioration of order is called entropy, and your home is not the only area of your life that can be affected. Remember:

"The natural drift of family life in contemporary America is toward slowly diminishing connection, meaning and community. You don't have to be a "dysfunctional"couple to feel more distant as the years go by, or a particularly inept parent to feel that you spend more time disciplining your children than enjoying them....Only an intentional family has a fighting chance to maintain and increase its sense of connection, meaning, and community over the years. An intentional family rows and steers its boat rather than being moved only by the winds and the current."[8]

If you are not intentional in trying to prevent entropy, your children, your relationships, your values, your life, or the world you live in, will eventually decay. Action and intent keep entropy at bay. When you see that the tree in the front yard is getting a little crazy, trim it back. When you notice something out of its place, take a few seconds to put it away. When you and Adam have a tiff, make time to sort things out. When you keep the prospect of entropy in the back of your mind, it is easier to stay ahead of the game.

Don't look back in disbelief, look forward and buckle up.

Love,
Me

---

[8] William J. Doherty, *The Intentional Family - Simple Rituals To Strengthen Family Ties* (New York: Avon Books), 8

Prioritization Step: Engineering Systems

We are surrounded by systems: whether it's the weather system or digestive, there is a degree of predictability based on what we already know about how the system works. For example, I know that if I drink a quart of chocolate milk my digestive system will become...aggravated. I know this from analysis of my own personal experience. This knowledge helps me have an easier time manipulating the things that I input to that system in particular. It is rare that I will have more than a gulp or two of milk because of what I know about my system.

Engineers design, build, run and continuously improve systems that produce desirable results. If a system isn't working quite right, an engineer will analyze it and change the inputs in order to get the level of performance desired.

Think of the medieval catapult. This is a system that was designed to channel potential energy. A rock can't do much on its own. The pull of gravity on it is constant though, and when that force is put to use, a significant amount of momentum is produced. I say it's time for us to engineer our lives and utilize the potential energy that is all around us.

I lived with a very aggravating laundry system for the first ten years of my marriage. As my husband and I added family member after family member, the situation became increasingly dire. We did our best, but there were often piles of clothing, clean and dirty, littering the hallways or frosting the top of our bed. It seemed that there was little we could do to contain the madness.

Upon seeing the small bedroom sized laundry space that we had in our new home, a friend suggested that we try the "family closet" thing. Re-engineering this system for our particular situation has not only contained, but nearly eliminated the aforementioned chaos.

The window inside the laundry room is deep, so we put up a curtain rod and have each child hang their tops on it. Underneath the window we placed a long, low dresser where each kid has a single drawer for pants or shorts. There are bins for socks and underwear, and pajamas go in the drawers of a taller dresser. The laundry room is the only area in our home where the children change their clothes. We even have a bathrobe hanging in this room for each child so that they can undress in the laundry room, put their robe on, run to the bathroom to shower, and then dry off on their way back to the laundry room to get fresh clothing.

There are two full-sized laundry baskets right next to the washing machine. White for whites and dark for colors. When a person changes clothes, they put their dirties straight into the appropriate basket and when the basket gets full, its contents will be washed and then dried. After drying, the clothes are dumped out onto the dresser under the window for sorting.

Now, in a perfect world, I would never find a stinky sock outside of the laundry baskets, or a crumpled t-shirt on a bedroom floor. It is not a perfect world (in case you hadn't noticed), which means that sometimes I walk into our laundry lair and find that the system has been overwhelmed. Because there is a system, though, I know exactly where to begin. I know that it isn't going to take me more than an hour and a half to get things working smoothly once more.

Having a system isn't the solution to every problem. Systems require individualized structure, supervision, and continuous improvement. You might feel overwhelmed by the prospect of engineering a system, but would that be any worse than the burden that you currently carry without one?

After designing a system, you'll need to keep in mind that you will likely have to make adjustments to your inputs based on your outputs. Maybe it kind of works but after a few months you realize that what you actually need is a housekeeper and a tighter budget.

Whatever your system is, make sure that it's working, that you like the way you do it, and that it fits your core beliefs and desires. Then move on to the next engineering project.

Take Action

Pick an area of your life that you would like to improve.

What is the desired result? Why do you want that result? If this area involves more people in your home besides yourself, and these people are capable of problem solving, invite them to be a part of this process.

Brainstorm. What is it about this particular thing that stresses you out or overwhelms you? What is the most extravagant solution that you can think of to this problem? What is the simplest? What would you do about this problem if there were no limitations such as time and money to consider?

Thinking things through in these extremes makes the improbable seem a little more realistic. Once you think of some crazy ideas, you may be able to see more clearly what actually needs to be done.

Make sure everything in this system has a place of belonging.

Determine the most logical sequence of events for this system.

Make the system as easy as possible to maintain.

Parent Trap:
Overlooking "Safety Belts"

Cars were invented in the late 1800's and were excitedly welcomed into modern society. The comforts and luxury that they provided were undeniable, however, increasing capabilities of cars made them progressively more physically dangerous. This is what prompted the invention of the safety belt.

From a study conducted in Sweden in the 1960's:

"Unbelted occupants sustained fatal injuries throughout the whole speed scale, whereas none of the belted occupants was fatally injured at accident speeds below 60 mph."[9]

The evidence has long indicated that the use of safety restraints in vehicles is effective. Even so, It has cost millions in campaigning, law enforcement citations, and far too many serious injuries and fatalities to get to our current seatbelt-wearing status. Today, we generally

---

[9] N. I. Bohlin "A Statistical Analysis of 28,000 Accident Cases with Emphasis on Occupant Restraint Value," SAE Mobilus, February 1, 1967, https://saemobilus.sae.org/content/670925/.

accept that using a safety belt while in an automobile is the wisest thing to do.

Cell phones are a tool much like cars. They help us get from point A to point B, but in relationships, in communication and in knowledge. Mobile phones were invented in the late 1970's. The speed and capabilities of cell phones have been steadily increasing since then, yet, many refuse to use any restraint while handling these beloved devices.

From a Forbes Article I recently read:

> *"Given that our brains can process about 120 bits per second, filters that help us choose which information to pay attention to are working overtime to determine what is and is not important to our survival. Sadly, shifts in what is "important" to developing minds also change how the brain filters information that affects our well-being. For example, teens are expressing higher rates of depression and loneliness the more time they spend on their phones – despite claims by 81% of teens that phones make them "feel" more connected."*[10]

---

[10] Nicole F. Roberts, "How Much Time Americans Spend In Front Of Screens Will Terrify You," Forbes, January 24, 2019, https://www.forbes.com/sites/nicolefisher/2019/01/24/how-much-time-americans-spend-in-front-of-screens-will-terrify-you/?sh=673b3d0e1c67.

Just as the car is physically dangerous, our favorite mode of intellectual transportation is a potential mental, social and emotional death trap. We can look at all of social media and internet use in this same light, and the evidence is all around us.

A dear friend and I were chatting about her younger two children. There's a ten year gap between the last two and the older three. Her older kids are in their thirties and the younger ones are just into their twenties. We spoke about the differences between raising those two groups, and talked about how both of her younger children struggle with anxiety and depression. The older three each had hard things to deal with but neither anxiety nor depression were among them. When I asked what the difference was her immediate answer was "cell phones." Her daughter explained: "you would be depressed too, if you saw the world the way I see it."

Every teenager goes to drivers ed before being let loose on the streets. There, they learn road laws and expectations and are taught the importance of using restraint. Since there are currently no federal mandates around cell phone and internet use, we as parents, must create safety belts for ourselves and our children.

Expectations about, guidelines for and appropriate uses of a phone and computer must be made clear to our kids. If we want to avoid the negative impacts of cell phone, social media and internet use we'll have to invent our own safety belts and then *use them*.[11]

---

[11] A lot of fascinating research has been done on kids and technology. These articles may help you formulate a training plan for cell phones and computer use in your home.

Katie Hurley, "Teenage Cell Phone Addiction: Are You Worried About Your Child?" PSYCHOM, October 21, 2022, https://www.psycom.net/cell-phone-internet-addiction

José De-Sola Gutiérrez, Fernando Rodríguez de Fonseca, Gabriel Rubio. "Cell phone Addiction: A Review" *Front Psychiatry,* 7 No. 175, (2016) doi: 10.3389/fpsyt.2016.00175

Michael Ungar, "Teens and Dangerous levels of cell phone use" Psychology Today, January 16, 2018, https://www.psychologytoday.com/us/blog/nurturing-resilience/201801/teens-and-dangerous-levels-cell-phone-use.

Take Action

Create your own family cell phone and "data" (internet use) plan.

When does a phone become a *necessary* tool for your children? What risks are associated with child cell phone and internet use?

What can you do to decrease the likelihood that your children will be negatively impacted by cell phone and internet use? What training can you give them and what fences can you put up that will help them exercise restraint with these tools?

Are there other areas of your life that you feel you and your family should be using safety restraints in? What are they?

Establish safety belts (boundaries and guidelines) for these areas to keep your family safe.

Chapter 6

Dear Crystal,

So, I understand that one of the kids is having a particularly tough time right now. You have been thinking about this issue incessantly, praying for him always, and you just don't see how things are going to work out. I feel to remind you: You are mother to more than just this one. How do you think the others are faring with a mother who is completely absorbed in something that she cannot control? Children are sensitive to every touch, and the lack of these touches are just as likely (or more) to leave lasting impressions. You have to remember the other children.

Even a thumb when held closely enough to your eye can block your view of the sun, so try and push it back a bit and get a more clear perspective.

Each and every one of them is struggling in their own way for many reasons. It's hard to be three! It's hard to be seven! Pick an age and there will always be a battle. Add to that the fact that they have a sibling who may not be making good choices, or who got really sick... their problems are only compounded. You have to free up some mind space in order to help them through this time as well.

Do something fun together. You're good at fun, don't let it be lost in your anxiety. Take time to consider the needs (not just physical ones) of each individual in your family and make time to ensure that these needs are being met. Talk to them, play with them, explain to them, and help them explore the many avenues that they have to receive support.

This is all going to work out. Let the worry subside so that you can be aware of ALL the things that are going on within the walls of your own home.

You've got this,
Me

Prioritization Step: Rotating Priorities

So, there are a lot of logistical details when it comes to my job as a parent. I already figured out what my core responsibilities are (back in chapter three), but what about all the "other" stuff that needs to happen? I can't spend all my time teaching, correcting and demonstrating principles, can I?

What about keeping the house clean or preparing good food? What about mowing the lawn and organizing the garage? What about my own personal care? There are many things other than the express teaching and rearing of children that are also part of my duty as a parent, but how can I know where to start?

While this next step is something that I tend to do intuitively, I can make greater strides in productivity with a little structure. It's not possible to do everything at once, so I do things one after the other: go to work, come home, eat, play, grocery shop, exercise and then go to bed. Sometimes I switch around my activities because immediate action is required. The slow drip under the bathroom sink turned into a waterfall, there aren't any clean socks, or I forgot to put a kid's lunchbox in his backpack. Now, the priority becomes fixing the leak, getting some laundry done and getting lunch to the school.

To avoid rushing from emergency to emergency, and to not leave things that are important to me unattended,

I have divided the auxiliary areas of my life into six basic categories (in no particular order) and put them on a "maintenance" rotation.

Keeping the House Clean: Bedrooms, laundry, bathrooms, school stuff, kitchen, ambient items (walls, blinds, windows, flooring, etc.), keepsakes / decor and shoes
Food: Meals / cooking, school lunches, grocery shopping, pantry / organization and food storage
Personal Care: Caring for my physical self, spiritual self, emotional self and relational / social self
Garage: Organization and accessibility of bikes and other recreational equipment, off season clothes, and all the other random stuff that we keep around
Yard: Lawn care and upkeep, weed removal, tree care, garden tending, etc.
Church: Assignments, service opportunities and responsibilities

If I were to put these six categories on a big wheel and didn't rotate it to the next category until the job was done, I'm pretty sure I would never get past Keeping the House Clean.

Instead, I think of my life as the insides of a clock: made up of many gears. Some are bigger than others, which means that they don't all rotate at the same speed. My Personal Care gear rotates quickly, I try to take care of those things daily, but my Yard wheel is much more relaxed. I don't need to mow the lawn or trim the trees quite as often. My maintenance rotation is pretty informal, I keep these categories posted, and when planning my day or week will do a quick look over to help me know where my effort is most needed.

Scheduling maintenance on the things that are important to you won't mean that you never have another emergency, but it will significantly decrease your levels of stress.

Since your life is different from mine, you get to decide which of your priorities need attention. Play around and see how many cogs you would like to make use of in your day, or which ones need a little extra time. Organizing your thoughts is going to make a big difference in organizing your life. You don't have to feel like you need to accomplish everything at once, just choose a few gears or items from within your gears to focus on for the day, and get rotating.

Take Action

Try this: Time yourself doing each of your tasks for one day.

How long did it take you to drop the kids off at school? How much time did you use getting yourself ready for the day? **Have your computer and phone keep track of how many minutes you spend using specific apps or websites.** How many of your twenty four hours were you at your job, and commuting to and from it? Did you spend any time with God? Were there times that you were able to employ more than one gear at a time?

Figuring out the amount of time you spend on each of your priorities will help you see where you can adjust. What time spending habits can you regulate so that you have a few more minutes (or hours) to put toward the things that you really desire?

Categorize your life so that all the important-to-you areas are covered.

Refer to these maintenance categories often so that you know where to focus your energy, and therefore, prevent neglected priorities from becoming emergencies.

Brainstorm ways that you can use all the "other" parenting responsibilities to teach, correct and demonstrate.

Every thing you do is an opportunity to parent. All of your other duties relate directly to your role as a parent: they are appendages to it. Use your appendages to support you through your greatest responsibility—parenting.

Parent Trap:
Hyper-focusing on "Fun" and "Now"

Turns out that in my case, dry lips is the first sign that I am not drinking enough water. I know I already told you that water is my favorite, but as a kid, I *hated drinking* water. I would much rather have had milk, juice, soda, squeeze-its, or a milkshake than take a sip of water. Water is so boring when compared to all the other exciting drinks around, which is exactly the kind of society we live in. We want everything to be fun, we want everything to be exciting and we want it right now. I don't want to have to wait for my body to absorb all the water that takes me forever to drink. I'd rather put that raspberry sherbet flavored chapstick on and enjoy soft, smooth and great tasting lips—right now. It's way easier for me to carry chapstick in my pocket (and deal with it going through the dryer on occasion) than to keep track of a water bottle all day and make sure that I drink what's in it.

Just last night, two of my boys were reluctant to go to a youth church event. Upon investigation, I learned that they didn't want to go because, "It's not going to be fun."

"Oh, so you don't want to go because you won't be having a Nerf gun war like last time? Or learning how to make cookies and then immediately eating every single one of them?"

You'd better believe that we had a very lively "discussion" (lecture) about fun and now. The activity that night was based around origami, which, granted, isn't as thrilling as chasing after each other with Nerf products, but think of all the skills that are required to excel in origami. Patience, precision, concentration, the ability to follow instructions…I could go on.

There's a problem with our society's hyper-focus on having fun and having it now. That is this: practically all of the things that develop quality characteristics in a human being fall into the "boring" category for many people, and they take *time*.

For example, How does one learn diligence? What about integrity? Hard work? Are these traits that a person is just born with and if you missed that handout then tough luck? No. These are traits that you can naturally be gifted in, but as with any character trait, they are also ones that can and should be acquired with a little time and effort. As parents, we can help our children develop these qualities by giving them opportunities to practice learning them over and over and over again. Let them learn a process and become proficient in it, like washing the dishes, folding the laundry, putting the ball in the upper left corner of the goal, playing scales, over and over and over. Let those fingers learn, no—memorize, every key and all the arpeggios even though that's not as "fun" as learning the latest hit song.

As a society we are and have been hyper focused on "fun" and "now" and it is coming back to bite us in the buns. We aren't encouraging hard work and diligence because we remember how we hated practicing the piano when we were kids and we don't want to bother with that fight. The result: our young adults are going into the world without as many quality characteristics as their counterparts of even twenty years ago.

I recently spoke with the owner of a small town movie theater (I'll call him Joe). He shared some interesting insights on the changes that he has observed in the three decades that his theater has been in business. Joe explained that thirty years ago someone who wanted a job would walk into the theater and ask for an application. Now it is difficult to find workers at all because "they want a job but they don't want to work."

We discussed how many of his young employees are not demonstrating much by way of personal responsibility. They don't know how to show up on time (or show up at all), are wanting time off for every little thing, and don't know how to talk on the phone.

Counting change and making eye contact, which were once commonplace abilities, are now rare commodities in a first time job holder.

We need to be doing more to prepare our children to succeed in a world where not everything that needs to be done is going to be fun. Just drink the water already!

Take Action

Involve children in day-to-day tasks. Point out the complications that come from avoiding or procrastinating "un-fun" duties.

Take time with each child to find out what their goals and dreams are - help them make plans to accomplish these things, support and encourage them to continue when they encounter difficulty along the way.

What activities do your children already participate in that are developing good character traits?

What expectations have you set for them?

Do they understand that not everything needs to be fun in order to be worthwhile?

What can you do to encourage them when things in life don't seem "fun"?

Chapter 7

Dear Crystal,

Congratulations! Nearly twenty years have passed and you've launched the last of your people into the world. They are all fantastic. You've been there for them and tried so hard to help them learn and grow without completely taking over their lives—phew! That was quite the ride. Now, they are off to a new life that's going to rock them to their core. This is the time that they get to test out all of the things that you've taught and it's going to be okay. I know at times it might seem like they didn't absorb a single thing from you…but trust me. They did. It's all in there somewhere and they'll find it, just give them a little time and space and love. They'll figure it out.

I'm guessing that there are a few conflicting emotions that you are trying to balance. This is a happy day in some ways but in others you feel a little bit sad. Happy that you are graduating to a new stage, sad that your role as mom will never be the same. Don't fret. There are many more opportunities to connect, lift and inspire in your future! Who knows, one of your kids might come back to live in the basement for a few years.

Maybe it feels like your motherhood is somehow diminished now that there is no one at home to be mother to, but you've got to put that out of your mind right now.

Your momdom only gets bigger from here. Daughters-in-law, grandchildren, and perhaps even unofficial adoptees. Don't make the mistake of buying into the idea that you are any less needed now that your own children don't live under the same roof as you—you're just needed in a different capacity, possibly even for different people and that's okay. In fact, it's more than okay–it's awesome.

Here's to finding out what that capacity looks like. You won't ever not be a mom, you still have responsibilities, so get to work!

Love,

Me

Prioritization Step: Deciphering Desires

Let me tell you about what happened to me just before I decided to write this book. I was feeling adrift. Lost in the sea of diapers, whining, crying and oatmeal. Lots and lots of oatmeal. My ship was listing and I could feel the unease in my daily doings. I recognized that I wasn't where I wanted to be and knew that *I had to be the one to initiate change.* I decided to write down all of the things that I desired from and out of life. I listed all of the things that I wanted to accomplish, all of the places I wanted to go, all of the skills I wanted to develop and all my deepest desires. After I had my list (it was a legal sized piece of paper and it was *jammed*), I sat there wondering how one person could want so much. No wonder I was feeling adrift - and writing it all out seemed to make things much, much worse!

As I sat there feeling overwhelmed and a little bit alone, I turned to God. I knew I needed His help to decipher my many desires. It was He who reminded me of something that I had lost sight of: my number one desire.

You know how sometimes you pick up a pen and it only leaves indentations on the page rather than ink? Yesterday, I picked up such a pen and spent a couple of minutes trying to coax the ink out. Eventually, I tossed it. I only grabbed that pen because my first choice was nowhere to be found.

My number one desire is to be a capable tool in the hands of God. I want to be the pen that doesn't need prodding, just a good, dependable instrument that doesn't leave clumps or take forever to dry. I'll be the .7mm Pilot G2 that's ready to address two thousand Christmas cards without complaint.

When I revisited that list with my ultimate desire in mind, I no longer felt overwhelmed or alone and I was able to focus. It wasn't hard to find my heading even through the turbulent sea of unfulfilled dreams and wishes. Do I want to be healthy? Yes. I want my body to be capable of service for as long as I am alive. Do I want to be wealthy? Definitely. I want to be able to give freely of the resources I am given to help God's work move forward. Do I want to be wise? Of course. I want to share the things that I have learned in hopes that others will come closer to Him.

"Master, which is the great commandment in the law?"

"Jesus said unto him, Thou shalt love the Lord thy God with all thy heart, and with all thy soul, and with all thy mind."[12]

Working toward my goals and dreams with this specific design behind them is how I live the first great commandment. I live my love for God.

He is my Priority Number One.

Take Action

We need to understand what we want, and more importantly *why* we want what we want. Do you have to have the same desires that I do? Nope, but however you structure it, if you choose to make God your first priority, things will fall into place more easily. This one principle will dramatically improve every area of your life, not just the parenting one.

Make a list of all the things you desire:

Where do you want to go? What do you hope for in your life? What childhood dreams did you have? What

---

[12] Matthew 22:36-37 (KJV)

do you want to accomplish? What do you want to become? What other bucket-list items do you have?

Why do you want these things? Are there any common themes among the items that you want to do?

Which of these desires seems most appropriate for the season of life that you are in? If you are currently rearing children, how do they fit into your desires?

Your true desires will lead you straight to who God created you to be, but you have to take the time to really know what they are and the why behind them.

Parent Trap: Assuming They Will Catch The Drift

One of the biggest traps that we can fall into as parents is to believe that our children are going to assume our values without effort and action on our parts. We tend to think that they learn by osmosis - values and knowledge will just seep into their souls because we are close in proximity. If you have ever thought "He should know better!" You may want to pause for a moment. Have you specifically taught your expectations on the matter? If you can't pinpoint the moment, or if you do remember that lesson but it was long, long ago…you may have fallen prey to "assuming they will catch the drift."

Take the specific value of hard work as an example. It used to be that nature was super helpful in teaching this principle. If you didn't work (hunt, gather, plow, milk the cow, etc), you could not feed yourself and would die. If you remember, the ground was cursed for Adam and Eve's *sake*. As in, it was a *good* thing for them to have to work. The ground still gives us goat-heads and tumbleweeds, but the great curse of our day is that the tie between work and alive-ness has been severed by the many different technologies that we enjoy.

Work is still a requirement of our physical bodies. Our social, emotional and spiritual selves are also being deprived when we don't work. If our children are going to learn hard work, we are going to have to work hard for it. This is not a one and done type of lesson, it's a life-long process of teaching, correcting, and demonstrating the principle.

Think of your religious beliefs. Do your children know how much you love God? Do they see you giving Him your time and best efforts? Are you regularly teaching them the principles that have guided you? If not, it may be time to wear your systems engineering hat.

The system in our home around prioritizing God and gospel involves regular church attendance, one set weeknight for the teaching of gospel principles, and daily scripture reading and prayer. Do these things happen every single time? No, but with the system in place and some effort to maintain that system, we show our children the love we have for God much more than we would otherwise.

Your best chance of having your children appreciate your values and establish similar ones of their own is for you to make them as tangible as possible. Teach the things that matter to you. Live the things that matter to you. Live them on purpose, and help your children understand why they matter so much to you. Remember that just because you taught something once, or even many times, doesn't guarantee that your charge was listening. Their mind may have been in a galaxy far, far away! You can only patiently teach time and time again.

Your influence isn't guaranteed just by the virtue of being a parent or being close in proximity. Children are not subjects and you are not their king. Just as a garden, if well tended, has a better chance of producing good fruit, so a child, if well reared, has a better chance of fulfilling his or her ultimate potential. Being a great gardener does not guarantee a great harvest, but a great gardener knows that the joy is found in *doing* a great work.

Take Action

Write down the values and principles that you hope your children will adopt into their own lives.

Which of these do you feel your children will benefit from the most? **Take into consideration the individual needs of each of your children, as well as their surrounding circumstances.**

What do you currently do that helps your children see how important these values are to you?

What more can you do to align your own life with your core values and beliefs?

Make goals and plans based on these answers.

Parting Words

When I was in first grade, my best friend and next-door neighbor's big sister won the Junior Miss competition in our hometown. It was awe inspiring to watch her wave to the crowd as she floated along the parade route in her beautiful dress and with her lovely smile. I was enamored and decided that I wanted to do that.

For the next ten years I worked hard in school, I kept myself physically fit, and when the time came closer I prepared my talent and even bought my dress. I signed myself up for the competition and had my picture taken for the newspaper: I was ready. A few weeks later each contestant was given a rehearsal schedule, and I was surprised to see that three of our meetings were to be held on a Sunday.

Usual Sunday activities for me up until that point in my life were attending church, spending time with family, and making cookies and then taking them to people. Our family always took the opportunity to use Sunday as a day of worship and rest. I decided to send a note to the program directors asking if it were possible for me to not attend those three Sunday sessions and still participate in the competition. I assured them that I was willing to practice at other times, happy to put in extra work, and would do everything that I could to make up for what I'd miss.

The reply I received was short and to the point.

"You need to get your priorities straight."

I was fully expecting that they would work with me on this. I had thought that I could pursue my dream while still honoring my values, but that's just not how it went down. My heart wasn't broken, it was decimated.

You know, it's interesting because—if the message had been "These practices are mandatory, sorry, you'll have to decide" or something to that effect—I think I might have chosen to participate. I wouldn't have felt any less faithful or like I was abandoning the things that I had been taught, it would just have been a choice. My parents would have supported me wholeheartedly, and everything would have been fine. But those words pierced my soul and I knew that I couldn't do it. Those words made the choice more than deciding between a "scholarship program" and enjoying a rejuvenating Sunday afternoon. I knew I didn't want to put anything before my commitment and dedication to God.

Competition day came, I cried through it, and then it was gone. Over twenty years have passed, and my life now is everything that I hoped for as a girl. Yes, that was a terrible time for my sixteen-year-old self, but I wouldn't trade it for the world. I'm grateful that it was made a matter of "getting my priorities straight," because it gave me cause to try the word of God. Even though I didn't get what I wanted, I felt His strength, His embrace and His love through it all. I even made good use of the dress I bought: I got married in it.

Whenever I was asked what I wanted to be when I grew up, I would say, "a mom!" It didn't take long to realize that that wasn't the answer people wanted to hear. So, I would say "doctor" or "nurse" instead and wait for the approving smiles. But in my heart and soul has always been the desire to "just" be mom. When the time came and my wish was granted, I spent many days wondering if being a "doc" would have been less complicated.

Yes. Parenting is full of challenges. Yes, we may or may not be avoiding the responsibilities that are ours as parents. And yes, our young people are struggling. We are struggling. Everyone is struggling—and it is going to be okay. While it is easy to become disheartened because parenting is so hard, we need to remember that the outcome of the struggle is completely up to us. We have the ability to turn what is tough into something tender, and we can do it through prioritization. We need to remember that *the struggle is why we are here* and that we are blessed with the hard things to make us better parents, and better people.

All of this is going to be right in the end because you are going to find your center. You are going to find the motivating purpose of your life right now. When you do, life will be full of excitement and adventure! It wouldn't be an adventure without those narrow escapes or moments of despair and hopelessness. If you can just find the will to overcome life's many challenges and the courageous determination to see it through, if you can make Him Priority Number One, that is where your exhilaration will begin!

~

Dear Nat,

You are almost 14 months old now and life is so good! You love the great outdoors, pulling things out of the fridge (especially raw eggs), and you love light switches. I can hold you next to a light switch and you'll be entertained as long as I can stand there!

Things are also a little bit tough. Your wants and needs have outgrown your ability to communicate them. With five older brothers, thus far you've been able to get what you want without using words—you lean in the direction you want to be taken, reach for items that you would like to examine with your hands, and squawk a little to get a person's attention. Lately, your wants are too specific for screeching and you have yet to learn that talking is a more effective way. It's hard.

Last night between dinner and bedtime was rough. You obviously wanted something but I had absolutely no idea what. It felt like I had tried everything I knew to do, but you were still unhappy. I did the only thing I could think of and just held you. We sat on the red couch in the office for a long, long time. You kicked, screamed and cried for almost half an hour but eventually you did settle down. I was surprised, even pleased, that not one of the boys came in looking for me during that time! I had the honor of serving you the best I could in your time of need for as long as you needed me. I thought about how God in his wisdom doesn't always give us what we want just because we want it. I would have given you whatever you desired had I just known what it was—but then, who knows, you might never learn to speak.

At times I wondered if you even knew that you were sitting on my lap! You were distressed and didn't seem to notice that I was wiping away your tears.

I hope that you will always remember that your Father (the one in Heaven) has got you. If you can keep your focus on Him you'll feel His support, His love and His understanding more freely. You will see clearly that He has been with you all along, and that He's not going anywhere.

I love you,
Mom

Dear Father,

I've been reflecting on the many things that I have to thank you for. First, I am thankful for experience. I hope that I have many years of experiencing things yet to come, but the lessons that I have already learned from the ups and downs of being alive are so beautiful.

Thank you for giving me the desire to make good use of said experience by writing a book.

Thank you for sending me to parents who taught me time and time again to look to you and live. Thank you for blessing me with children who so effortlessly push me to the very edge of my capabilities and fill every quadrant of my heart with love. Thank you for giving me a partner who cares just as deeply as I do about the life that we are creating together, and who is always supportive of my wildest dreams.

Thank you for helping me build relationships and enabling me to maintain them even though distance and a pandemic have been doing their best to keep me feeling alone. Thank you for sending me Shelly. When I was overburdened and overwhelmed with the task of writing a whole book, she took some of my load and I was able to move forward again. Thank you for Becky, Christi, Emily M, Emilee, Jessica, Emily G, Courtney, Koria, ShaNeill, Chante', Brad, Evan, Mary Ann, Grandpa and Grandma, Mom and Dad. Each of them endured reading my early drafts and gave feedback and encouragement freely. Thanks for Chloe. She was exactly what was needed to wrap this project up beautifully.

Thank you for putting me in contact with so many people who had experiences with older kids that I needed to hear about in order to sort out my own parenting thoughts and feelings. Thank you for Jami, Jan, Cheryl, Bob and Eric. Their insights and experiences were foundational to the development of this book. Thank you for connecting me with Kerry; she has trained me to take my thoughts by the reins, which has helped me in every area of life. Thank you for all the good parents that I have been close enough with to observe, and the friends and family who have been there and done that (or are there and doing it). I have learned so much from the examples and experiences of those around me.

Thank you for helping me to finally consider myself a writer. You gave me all the technical help I needed in order to feel successful in this field. Thank you for sending me Gina. She has been so supportive of my ideas and has helped me see things about my work that I never would have been able to discover on my own. Thank you for giving me mentors like Grandpa and Patrick who each offered so much help by asking good questions. Thank you for giving me the fire I needed to begin this grand adventure and for placing people around me who knew better than to dump water all over my unrealistic goals and expectations.

Thank you for preparing The Way for us all to be cleansed from our sins and come home. Thank you for letting us live, learn and love our way through life. I imagine at times we are frustrating, so thank you for being patient and kind. And thank you for never letting us cry alone.

I love you and am forever grateful,
Crystal

Works Cited

Bohlin, N. I. "A Statistical Analysis of 28,000 Accident Cases with Emphasis on Occupant Restraint Value," SAE Mobilus, February 1, 1967, https://saemobilus.sae.org/content/670925/.

Doherty, William J. "The Intentional Family" In *The Intentional Family: Simple Rituals To Strengthen Family Ties,* 8. New York: Avon Books, 1997.

Gutiérrez, José De-Sola, Fonseca, Fernando Rodríguez de, Rubio, Gabriel. "Cell phone Addiction: A Review" *Front Psychiatry,* 7 No. 175, (2016) doi: 10.3389/fpsyt.2016.00175

Janson, Chris. "Buy Me A Boat" Track 1 on *Buy Me A Boat.* Warner Records, 2015, CD.

Ray, Brian D. "How Many Homeschool Students Are There In The United States During the 2021-2022 School Year?" National Home Education Research Institute. September 15, 2022, https://www.nheri.org/how-many-homeschool-students-are-there-in-the-united-states-during-the-2021-2022-school-year/).

Roberts, Nicole F. "How Much Time Americans Spend In Front Of Screens Will Terrify You," Forbes, January 24, 2019, https://www.forbes.com/sites/nicolefisher/2019/01/24/how-much-time-americans-spend-in-front-of-screens-will-terrify-you/?sh=673b3d0e1c67.

Works Cited

Ungar, Michael. "Teens and Dangerous levels of cell phone use"
        Psychology Today, January 16, 2018, https://
        www.psychologytoday.com/us/blog/nurturing-resilience/
        201801/teens-and-dangerous-levels-cell-phone-use.

Wikipedia. "List Of People Who Have Gone Over Niagra Falls."
        Accessed Jan 28, 2023, https://en.wikipedia.org/wiki/
        List_of_people_who_have_gone_over_Niagara_Falls

Zero To Three. "Tuning In: National Parent Survey Report."
        Accessed Jan 28, 2023, https://www.zerotothree.org/wp-
        content/uploads/2022/10/National-Parent-Survey-
        Report.pdf

Dear You

We don't connect as often or as readily as we should. We rely on social media to give us a sense of togetherness, yet we are apart. When we need help we reach out to the universe in general rather than picking up our phone and giving someone a call.

There is a huge resource that we aren't tapping into as parents: the experience of other parents. Our diminished real-life circles are such that we might not even be able to find the help we need within them! I'd like to help change that. My husband and I are working on a project that will make the knowledge and real-life experience of other parents more easily accessible, and we'd love for you to join us.

If you are interested in continuing the parenting conversations that have been started in this book, or want additional support along your own parenting journey then we want to be there for you. You are not alone in this struggle!

Hope to connect with you soon,
Crystal
www.prioritynumberone.org

Crystal Rita (Gerber) Zurligen has a bachelor's degree in recreation management and youth leadership. This has definitely come in handy raising her five (soon to be six) sons and one daughter. She loves to throw a great party, has a deep and abiding faith in God, enjoys coaching her children's soccer teams, and is an extraordinary friend.